The Winter Goose

by Duncan Searl
illustrated by Oki Han

In a great, gray *V*, the geese fly south. Fat drops of rain splash against their feathers. A cold wind whistles by. "Honk, honk," the geese sing to each other. *Stay in line, stay in line.*

Miles below, people hear the music of the geese. "Listen!" they say. "The geese are flying south. Winter is on the way."

Winter is on the way, and so are the geese. It is late October, and the fall days are getting shorter. A week ago, the geese left their summer nests in Canada. Now they are on their way to Mexico—2,500 miles (4,032 km) away!

The geese are flying fast now—over 48 miles (77 km) per hour. Already today they have flown 150 miles (241 km). A young goose at the end of the *V* flaps her wings harder. This is her first trip south. It isn't easy to keep up.

"Honk, honk." *Down there, down there.* The birds spot water and a cornfield. They glide lower around the lake and splash down. It is time to eat and rest.

The young goose follows the flock into the cornfield. Farmers have already picked the corn, but bits of corn cover the ground.

There is also danger on the ground. The geese know danger, so two of the older birds of the flock stand guard. They have made the long trip many times. They know what to watch for while the others eat.

The young goose is hungry, and the corn is sweet. Head down, she pecks the yellow grain. Farther and farther across the field she moves.

"HONK! HONK!" *Take off! Take off!* The older birds see a danger. With a flash of wings, the flock rises in a cloud.

Too late! The young goose hears the cry too late. "Honk, honk!" she cries. *The danger has me.* She tries to fly, but it bites her wing. She tries to rise, and her wing snaps.

"Toby! Toby! No! Put it down!" Now a second danger stands above the goose. "Look what you've done, Toby." The young goose struggles to take off but flops over on her broken wing.

The frightened goose is wrapped inside a woolly nest and lifted up. She tries to flap wildly. But the nest is tight around her. "Don't worry, little goose," says a voice. "Don't worry." High above, the *V* flies away.

The last brown leaves fall from the trees. The first snow drifts down. From a pen in a barn, the young goose watches the gray sky. She listens for the familiar honking. Now the silent sky is empty except for snow. Her flock is far away.

Time passes slowly for the young goose. She looks outside and sees that the snow covers the grass and the trees. Inside, the goose's broken wing is taped tightly to a stick. When she tries to fly, she falls back on the floor.

Thousands of miles south in Mexico, the flock finds its winter home. Along the beach of a

bay, the geese build grassy nests. Here the grass grows all winter, and the warm water is alive with insects. After their long trip, the geese rest all winter in the sun.

Each morning, the woman brings corn and water to the pen. At first, the wild bird backs away in fear. Sometimes she hisses angrily or tries to peck the woman's legs. Only when the woman leaves does she eat the food. As the weeks go by, the goose learns to trust the woman. Sometimes she lets the woman pick her up.

One day, the woman frees the goose's wing from the stick. The goose stretches and flaps her wing. Up, out of the pen, she flutters. Up to the barn roof she flaps. Then she drops down again. Flying—she is almost flying!

On a sunny day in March, the young goose sees water dripping from an icicle that hangs from the roof. Another day, she looks outside and wonders where the white fluffy snow has gone. Some small birds fly through the barn one morning. One night, an old skunk wakes from her winter sleep and wanders past the pen.

It is spring now, and the goose stays outside the barn. Her wing is getting stronger. Each day she circles over the lake and cornfield. Watching the sky and listening, the young goose waits.

At last they come! With a noisy flapping, the flock lands in the lake beside the cornfield. The goose flies out to meet them. "Honk! Honk!" she cries. *I missed you.*

The woman watches the geese fly north. To the goose at the end of the *V* she calls, "Good-bye, my winter goose. I'll miss you."

In May the geese reach their summer home. The long spring journey north is over. The flock will stay in Canada all summer long.

The goose has a mate now. The goose makes a nest of moss and grass and lays three white eggs. Taking care of the three goslings is her summer job.

By fall, the baby goslings will have grown into young geese. When the cold winds begin to blow, they will be big enough to fly far. The family will join the flock to make the long trip south.